More Treasured Stories *of the* War Between the States

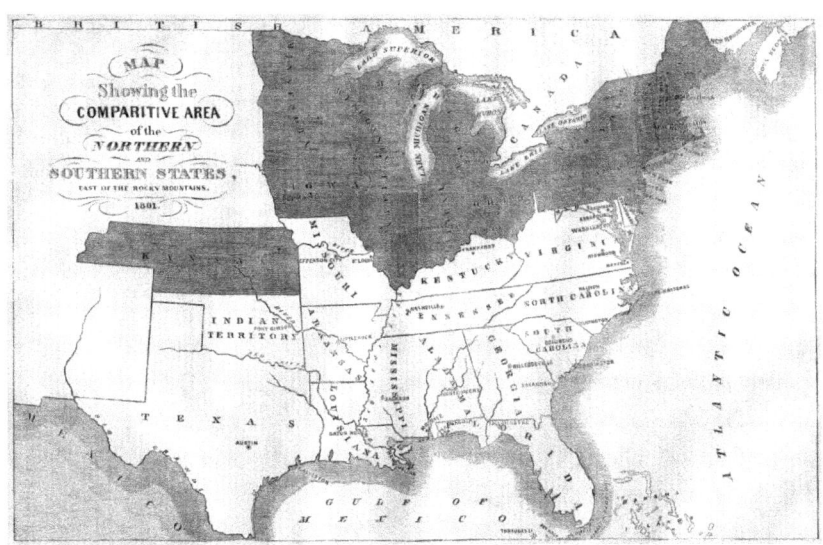

Dr. Tony Zeiss

Wake Forest, NC
www.scuppernongpress.com

More Treasured Stories of the War Between the States
Dr. Tony Zeiss

Copyright © 2024 Dr. Tony Zeiss

Second Printing

The Scuppernong Press
PO Box 1724
Wake Forest, NC 27588
www.scuppernongpress.com

Cover and book design by Frank B. Powell, III

All rights reserved.
Printed in the United States of America.

No part of this book may be reproduced or transmitted in any form or by any means, electronic or mechanical, including photocopying, recording, or by any information and storage and retrieval system, without written permission from the editor and/or publisher.

International Standard Book Number
                          ISBN 978-1-942806-68-4

Library of Congress Control Number: 2024941493

Table of Contents

Introduction	iii
I've Had Enough Fightn'	1
I Always Take My Coffee Black!	3
Two Diaries	5
Self Preservation: A Strong Instinct	7
Curious Things	11
Don't Break Army Rules	13
Misery and Luck	17
He Returned A Hero with A New Name	19
A Glimpse of Loneliness	21
A Strong Willed Woman	23
A Family Coincidence	25
Homesick Horse	27
Mama Stayed Angry Till She Died	29
Brotherly Love	31
Grandma's Missing!	33
Two Brothers and A Ghost	35
Kindness Prevailed	37
Nothing Was Safe	39
The Survivor	41
Execution of A Deserter	43
Henry's Letter	45
Love's A Powerful Motivator	47
Eye Witness at Gettysburg	49
The Money Dress	51
Surprise Pillow	55
Desperation	57
A Southern Woman's Grit	59
Divine Intervention	63
Fraternal Ties Are Strong	67
An Old Man In A No-Win War	73
A Yankee Prisoner In Texas	75
About the Author	77

Introduction

The intent of this book is to preserve an important part of our county's history. Each story featured here originated from eye witnesses of the War Between the States and has been passed down through two, three, and sometimes four generations. These, however, are the stories that the participants choose to pass on to their children and grandchildren. They are worthy of preservation in their own right, but more importantly, they present a vivid picture of what that trying time in our history was really like, from the ordinary person's experience.

Every effort was made to insure historical accuracy, but specific facts regarding the incidents portrayed in these family gems were often sketchy and incomplete. It is hoped these treasured vignettes, often the only link between twentieth century families and their ancestors who participated in the War, will be enjoyed by people who wish to catch a glimpse of that historic period.

This book is the second of its kind. The first is titled *Treasured Stories of the War Between the States*. Please enjoy.

— *Tony Zeiss*

I've Had Enough Fightn'
As told by Sharon High

This story about Mrs. High's great grandfather gives us an insight to the terrible effects of the War Between the States.

Raiford Pearce fought in the war with Mexico as a teenager so it was no surprise that his patriotism would be rekindled when he learned that North Carolina had finally seceded from the Union. Even with a wife and five daughters, Raiford quickly enlisted in Company C of the Twenty-forth regiment of the North Carolina Volunteers.

In short order, Raiford was in the thick of battle. He fought in nearly all of the Western Virginia battles and against General George McClellan's Peninsula campaign. It was during the battle of Malvern Hill that Raiford was captured and sent to a prison camp in New Jersey. He was lucky to be in a prisoner exchange within one month and returned to his old unit where he resumed his old duties. He soon fought at Harper's Ferry, Sharpsburg (Antietam), and Fredricksburg. He was granted leave to visit home in Goldsboro, North Carolina in January, 1863. Unfortunately, he found his wife and children were in a terrible condition.

His wife had contracted Tuberculosis, a death sentence in those days. His young daughters were in a sad condition with little to eat and no one to care for them. Raiford took the only reasonable course of action. He deserted from the Confederate army. In September, Raiford was captured by the provost guards and taken back to Virginia. The penalty for desertion, of course, was death. He was imprisoned in a small log cabin, which had only a door and a window in front. All he could think about was his poor family. On the night before he was to be hanged, Raiford climbed up the small chimney and escaped. He ran and walked all night through the countryside, careful to avoid being detected.

At the break of day, he came upon the James River which was about two miles across at that point. Despite his fatigue, he began swimming away from the Confederate camps to the other side of the river. After what seemed like all day, Raiford finally reached the opposite bank and collapsed. After awhile, he opened his eyes to see a Yankee on a horse staring down at him.

"Hey soldier, where do you think you're going?" the Yankee asked.

"I'm going home just as hard as I can!" The Union soldier laughed and replied: "Well, go on your way then." Raiford wasted no time in leaving.

POST NOTE: Raiford made his way back to North Carolina to find that his wife had died. As a fugitive from the army, he could not easily care for five young girls. He parceled the children to good homes and left the area until after the war. He lived a long life and died in 1918.

I Always Take My Coffee Black!
As told by Robert Zeiss

Calvin Carey, grandfather of Robert Zeiss and a veteran of the 17th Indiana Light Artillery, often shared this explanation for the reason he always drank black coffee:

Eighteen year old Calvin had been through several days of difficult marching with his unit and others under General Sheridan in the famous Shenandoah Valley campaign of 1864. The purpose of this offensive was to push the Confederates out of the valley and destroy their major route for northern aggression. The mission was to confiscate or burn all the crops, stored provisions, and live stock in the valley.

During the march into the valley Calvin and his friends had no time to build fires during the day and were forbidden to build them at night fearing the enemy would discover their presence.

"After a few days," Grandfather Carey would explain, "we boys got an awful craving for hot coffee. In fact, it became the major topic of discussion and complaints. Finally, our unit was given a full hour for lunch. We fell out next to a dusty road bordered on the left by woods and on the right by a pasture. My messmates and I quickly gathered some small sticks and built a fire to boil water for coffee. We could taste that coffee just thinkin' about it. In short order the ground coffee was thrown into a pail of boiling creek water. The aroma was just wonderful and we all had our tin cups ready for active duty."

"I had just one problem," Calvin would state. "I preferred my coffee with cream. When we were bivouacked all those months back near Washington City, cream was in great supply. But down there on the march, there seemed little prospect for cream. Just then I saw a lone milk cow step into sight in that pasture we were sittin' beside. Without another thought, I proudly told my messmates I'd be having cream in my coffee. They scoffed as someone poured the steaming elixir into my cup, but I climbed over the rail fence and walked straight for that old cow."

"Having been raised around milk cows all my life, I knew how to approach her. She was a bit skittish, since I was a stranger, but I was determined to get a squirt of milk or my pals would never let me forget it. After a minute or two of soft talking, I got her confidence and was pleased to see her udder was fairly full. Just as I thrust the cup under her, a Confederate cannon fired at us from a hill above the pasture. That cow kicked and jumped like the devil was in her. She spilled my coffee and I hotfooted it back to my unit to get our battery into action. We fought off and on for nearly two days during which I never got another chance for a cup of coffee. After that," Grandfather Carey stated with conviction, "I always took my coffee black!"

Two Diaries
From an 1897 manuscript by William M. Thomas

Adjutant William Thomas was attached to Confederate General Johnson Hagood's brigade which fought in the trenches of Petersburg, Virginia and in the woods and fields of Cold Harbor, Virginia. He saw plenty of action during his tour of duty and he recorded it all in a diary. It was his hope the diary would someday prove useful as an historic record of his brigade.

In late January of 1865 an order was given to grant leaves to all officers who had been on duty for a year. One provision, however, prevented more than one officer to be absent at a time. William's detailed diary offered proof to his commanding officer he met the time requirement and qualified for a leave along with one other officer, Lieutenant E. B. Bell. William was first in line to take his leave, but E. B. Bell persuaded William to change the order of the leaves because his wife was ill. After thirty days or so, Lieutenant Bell returned and William was allowed to visit his home near Winnsboro, South Carolina. William's colonel recognized the value of recording the historical incidents of the brigade, instructed William to leave his diary with Lieutenant Bell who would act as temporary adjutant until William's return and keep the diary current.

The bloody battle of Bentonville, North Carolina erupted while William was on leave. During this battle, his colleague, E. B. Bell was killed. Bell's body was never recovered and William's diary was lost forever. William mourned the loss of the diary as well as his friend.

Some thirty-two years later, William was excited to learn that a fellow officer, Adjutant George Moffett had also kept a diary and that it might yet exist. After much research, William was able to get Moffett's diary and copy it. This diary closely replicated the events listed in William's lost diary.

Adjutant Moffett's diary had an unusual course of its own. Just before William's leave of absence back in 1865, Adjutant

Moffett had given William a package of articles to take home to his wife. Unknown to William, that package contained Moffett's diary. William dropped the package at the end of the rail line in Chester, South Carolina for Moffett's wife to pick up. Before she could retrieve it, some of General Sherman's Union cavalry raided Chester and took away everything that wasn't nailed down, including Moffett's package and his diary. Meanwhile, those same raiding federals rejoined their general in time for the battle of Bentonville.

After the battle, some of Adjutant Moffett's men recovered his diary from a dead Union soldier and returned it to the astonished officer. Thirty-two years later, William learned about the diary and his role in its strange course. Thus, at the same time and place William's precious diary was lost, Adjutant Moffett's diary was found. The historic record of General Hagood's brigade was preserved after all.

Self Preservation: A Strong Instinct
From the diary of H. B. Peterson

Young H. B. Peterson had traveled all the way from the state of New York to participate in the glories of battle. It didn't take him long to realize there was very little glory in war. It was 1862 and he was with Company K of the 27th regiment, New York volunteers. They were part of Union General George B. McClellan's offensive down in the Virginia peninsula. The following incidents recorded by Peterson offer a true to life glimpse into the trials of the privates during that campaign.

"This has been the longest day I ever knew. Early this morning I crept out beyond our lines, which were in the woods, to get a 'shot' (at a Rebel) before breakfast. But the Rebels spied me and everyone within shooting distance opened on me. The consequence was that I had to stay behind a tree all day until dark. The sun was awful hot and I didn't have a mouthful to eat or drink. The soldiers on both sides were yelling at me: 'Do you want some water?' old Butternut would ask. 'Well, we have a kettle on the fire heating for you,' my friends would say.

On another occasion young Peterson was ordered to help build a bridge across the Chickahominy and the mud was waist deep. "I tried at first to keep away from the mud and succeeded admirably until the Rebels threw some shells at us which came so close I was glad to lay low on the bosom of Mother Earth. No one was hurt in our party, but one man was killed near us."

Rain and mud seemed to plague the boys on the Peninsula campaign. Peterson describes a typical camp scene: "Away we went again in the night leaving the rifle pits without receiving any good from our hard work throwing them up. We followed the banks of the river down ten miles under the protection of the gunboats and went in camp in a large wheat field. We just got our tents pitched when it commenced to rain and it never ceased all night. The whole army is encamped in the field, which is only a few inches above the level of the river. We are almost under water. I went to Harrison's landing where there was a large quantity of provisions. I got all I could carry inside as well as out and the consequence is I feel better already. The mud was so deep I had to throw away one large ham. I lost both my shoes while I was in the river washing off."

While on picket one day about three miles from camp, Peterson met the commanding general McClellan. In his words: "The ground we occupy has deep ditches plowed in it by the shells from the gun boats." It also supported an abundance of blackberries which were nearly as large as butternuts. "The berries were a great luxury to me when served with sugar. General McClellan rode out to the lines to mark out a place for a fort or rifle pits. I had the honor of a short conversation with him. I presume my hat full of nice berries tempted him to speak to me — but he didn't get any."

Some terrible things happened to each combatant of that war. Peterson tells about one of his own: "We were pushed into the fight on a double quick and made a charge driving the Rebels from behind some houses. We took possession since the houses protected us. I left my gun and bayonet in the old house pinning a Rebel. It happened this way. I went in to clean my gun when I saw him taking aim at me. I made a thrust and had to leave as we were falling back to our old camp. How I escaped is to me a wonder. When the bullets were flying so thick and boys were falling all around me."

Fortunately, some lighthearted distractions helped to keep it all in balance. Peterson made this entry in his diary on July 17th, 1862: "It is uncommonly hot after the rain of last night. The flies are eating me up alive. They are perfectly ravenous. I made a great slaughter among them by placing some powder and sugar together then ignited the powder which left my quarters without any wings crawling around!"

Another diary entry describes more Yankee ingenuity: "We do guard duty by companies now and the company officers are held responsible for everything missing in the commissary. So much of the fresh meat was gone the other night and whiskey too. I hope this new method will stop the thefts. I know of four canteens being filled even when the lieutenant was sitting on the whiskey barrel. They bored a hole in the side of the barrel. Some sugar and coffee was also lugged off in an old pair of drawers."

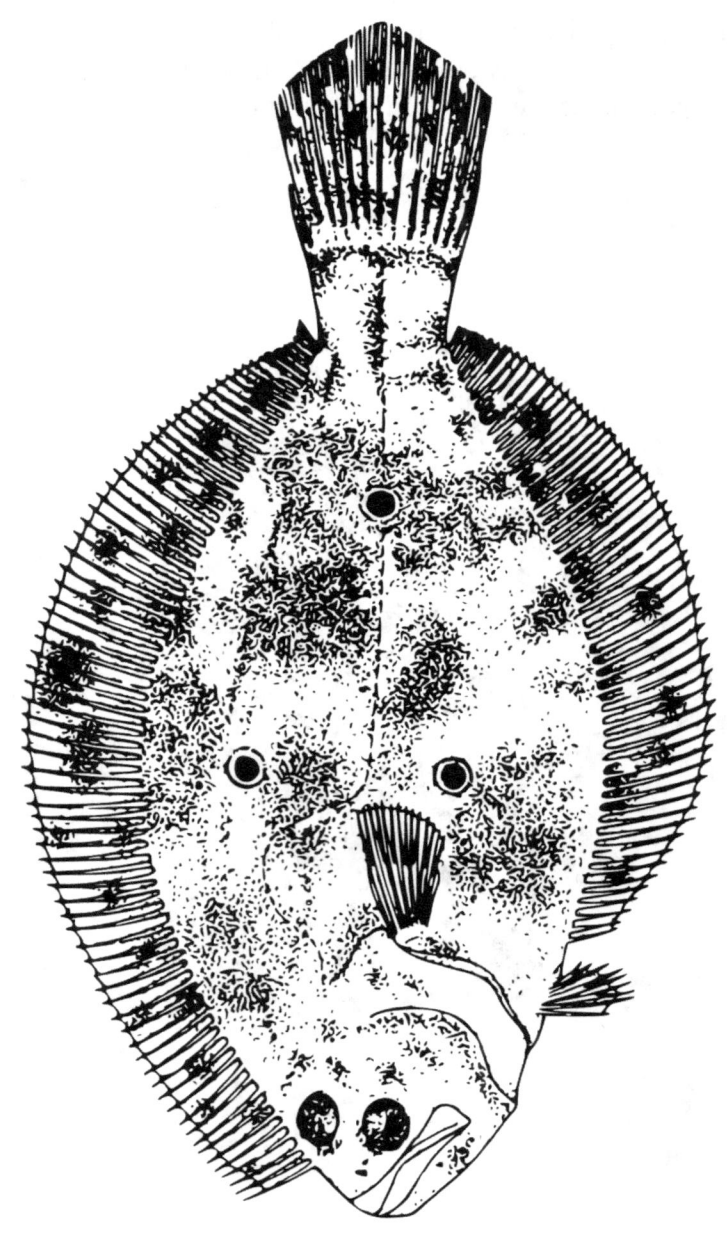

Curious Things
Excerpts from a *Confederate Veteran* publication, April, 1908

In April 1861, Jimmy Reese, of Edneyville, North Carolina, volunteered with a company called the Edney Greys. Jimmy and his pals had never been outside of Henderson county, North Carolina and they learned much as they moved all over the south during the war.

Jimmy's first duty station after training in the North Carolina Mountains, was near the coastal town of Wilmington, on Mitchel's sound. On the first morning there, Jimmy witnessed "… a fusillade of words and oaths exchanged between two mess mates about their coffee. Each accused the other of putting salt in his coffee cup. They had taken water from the sound, which they thought was a river! The boys were soberly informed the Atlantic Ocean was salty."

Shortly after their breakfast, an old man selling fish approached Jimmy and his friends. "Among the lot," noted Jimmy, "was one fish that appeared to be deformed. One side was white, with the other black, and both eyes were on one side of its head. When we called the old man's attention to this, he said: 'O, that fish is a Flounder.' Lump Freeman asked where in the world had that fish been 'floundering' to get himself into such a shape!"

Jimmy Reese learned many other curious things during his tour of duty as a Confederate soldier. One of the most curious was experienced while he was camped somewhere below Richmond, Virginia between the James and Appomattox rivers. It seems both armies were entrenched within sight and hearing distance and the pickets would fire at each other on sight. "They would get up a hot firing and Minie balls would fly thick for awhile. Then some Yankee would say in an undertone: 'Johnnie, if you will meet me halfway, I will give you some good coffee for some good Dixie tobacco.' We always found Mr. Yankee as good as his word. But when the exchange was over, he would say:

'Now Johnnie, we had better get back to our places before an officer comes.' The officers would quarrel and threaten punishment when they discovered we'd been trading with the Yankees, but they would drink the cup of real coffee with great enjoyment and read the Yankee newspapers with interest!"

Don't Break Army Rules
Excerpts from the diary of James W. Howard

In July of 1861, twenty-five year old James Howard joined Company A of the ninth Arkansas regiment at Pine Bluff. It wasn't long before James clearly understood the importance of strong military discipline. In less than a month, his captain was arrested for disobedience. Six days later the same captain was 'bucked and gagged' for striking an officer. Bucking consisted of setting a man down, tying his hands together and slipping them over his knees. A stick was then run through the space beneath the knees and over the arms. Gagging was accomplished by tying a stick or bayonet into one's mouth. This procedure usually went on eight hours a day for thirty days.

In December, James' company built winter quarters at Camp Beauregard. While there, three men from another regiment got drunk and robbed an old woman and her two daughters. James reported "The women came to camp, hunted the three out and reported them to their colonel. They were proved to be the guilty ones and were court martialed and sentenced to leapfrog around a bullring for one hour and rest four hours. Then they had to leap one hour and rest four more and so on. The bullring was thirty feet in diameter and was made by driving stobs into the ground six feet apart. The stobs were eighteen inches high with boards two feet long laid across them, flat on the top. They had to do this for thirty days living on bread and water the whole time. They had to leap over the boards at the tap of a drum with a bayonet close behind them. Often they would faint. When the thirty days were out, the whole division was called out and formed into a hollow square. The three men were then stripped to the waist and had their heads shaved. They were marched around close in front of all the men so all could see them well. Three stacks of arms were made and each man was tied to one. Then ten musicians were ordered to give each man ten licks with a horsewhip. The bass drummer was last to come and he was ordered to cut the skin at every lick while the first man was told to strike lightly. They cried out with pain at every blow. The twelve guards who had been guarding them with fixed bayonets double quicked them out into the woods and left them."

In various other places in his wartime diary, James reported witnessing executions. One particularly sad event was recorded: "I saw two deserters from our regiment shot. The rule is that when a man deserts, twelve men are drawn from his company to execute sentence. They are drawn alphabetically and it so happened that one of the men drawn was a brother to one of the deserters. When the captain learned this he told the drawn brother he would be excused. The brother said that he didn't want to be excused from his duty. He said he had tried to keep his brother from deserting and wanted justice done. He went on, but of course he didn't know whether he shot his brother or not as six of the guns were loaded and six shot blanks."

On at least two occasions James was authorized to serve as temporary Provost guards to track down deserters. Once he and two colleagues had to walk thirty-six miles on a railroad track, but they caught their deserters and returned them. James said he couldn't sleep all night for seeing cross ties jump up before his eyes.

On another occasion, James disarmed a local bandit and turned him over to the military authorities. When the notorious bad guy was asked if James took him all alone, the bandit replied; "Yes! That fool would have shot me!"

Justice also prevailed for spies. On one such occasion, during the fighting around Vicksburg, Mississippi, James' unit captured a federal spy. James wrote that the spy was sentenced to be executed at three in the afternoon: "… so the enemy asked for an armistice from two to four (o'clock) as they wanted to send some of their men over to find out particulars, be present at the execution, and take charge of the body. This was granted and the Federals were present. While this was going on, the men decided to meet on half way ground and have a social chat. The man whom I met and talked to was a handsome man with a black beard. His beard was just full of dirt and I asked him what was he doing with all that dirt in his whiskers. He said 'You Rebs shoot so close we have to get down and bite the dirt!' He laughed heartily. I asked him if he was a member of the church and he said yes, that he was a Baptist. I told him that I was one too and he said it was very nice Baptists we were, fighting each other. We both said if it was left to us, we would not fight. At four o'clock we had to go to fighting again, this continued all night."

Misery And Luck
Exerts from a letter by William J. Clarke

William Clarke of New Bern, North Carolina left his wife Mary and three children, Tom, Willie, and daughter Pet, to serve as an officer for the Confederacy. He suffered the same hardships as his troops. In his July, 1862 letter to Mary he reported: "I have been almost starved for we have had nothing to eat but very salty bacon and crackers, with no tea or coffee most of the time. I thought I had seen something of hardship, exposure and fatigue before, but I was mistaken. We left Petersburg with only a change of clothes and very soon were separated from that and I went two weeks without changing my shirt. The men carried knapsacks, but had to leave them and take only a blanket; then they had to leave the blanket and sleep in the open air during some very cold nights with no covering. I carried an oilcloth and a blanket behind my saddle, but was compelled to leave my horse and sleep without any covering. The night before our last battle, the army shelled us so severely that we had to send our horses to the rear. Mr. Cooke and I lay together on some hickory and cedar twigs which I cut down with my knife. We became so cold during the night that we had to hug each other to keep warm."

On the other hand, William was fortunate indeed to avoid capture or death when he rode beyond the lines into enemy territory. This day, luck, rather than misery, was with him. He wrote of the occasion: "You can tell Tom that Bill (William's horse) saved father from being taken prisoner. On the night of the 25th, I volunteered to go to Colonel Vance with an order and got lost and went among the enemy. We had not gone far before a heavy firing commenced and the bullets fairly rained around me. Bill carried me out like an arrow and made some extraordinary leaps. He has learned to stand fire pretty well."

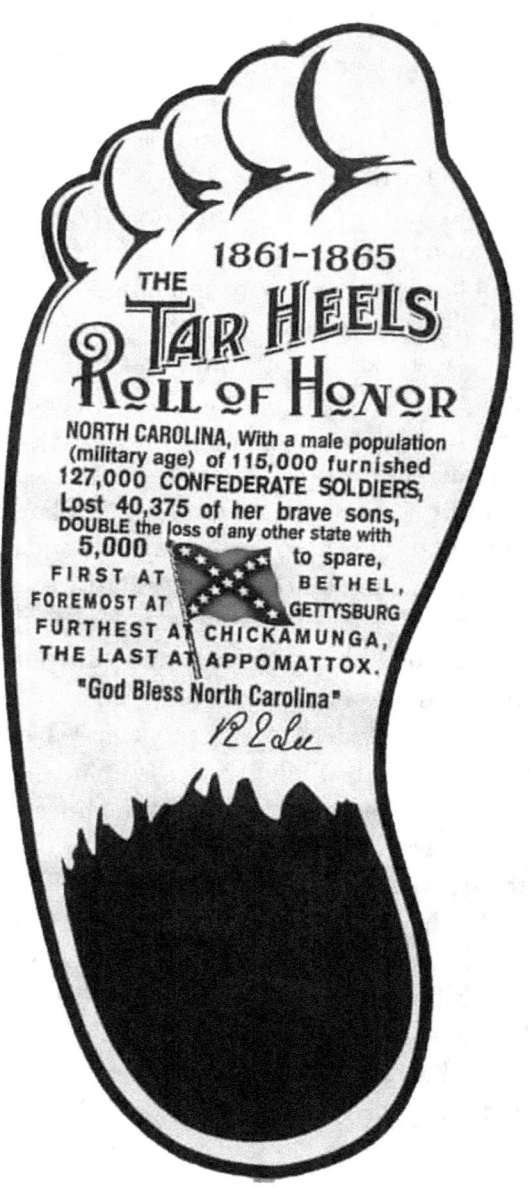

He Returned A Hero With A New Name
Provided by Mrs. Frank Dowling

Twenty-year-old Stephen Marks, from Steel Creek, North Carolina, enlisted as a private in Company B, Thirteenth North Carolina Infantry Regiment in April, 1861. Like most new recruits, he was fearful the fighting would be over before he could participate. He shouldn't have worried about it. Before his four long years of duty were over, Steven saw plenty of action and came home a hero with a new name.

In the terrible battle of Sharpsburg (Antietam), September 17, 1862, Steven was wounded in the arm. He recovered in time to see action in several more battles before fighting at Gettysburg the following July. In one of these fights, Stephen got into hand to hand fighting. He somehow unlocked the bayonet from one foe's rifle and took him prisoner. In the meantime, the Yankees surrendered. Stephen's superiors reportedly allowed him to do whatever he wanted with his prisoner. Stephen took his prisoner into the deep woods and returned without him. To his dying day, March 29, 1917, what Stephen did with his prisoner remained a mystery.

It was in the battle of Gettysburg where he distinguished himself by exhibiting uncommon valor. His regiment, like most North Carolina regiments, was favored by General Robert E. Lee to lead the way in battle. In a second-day charge, Stephen's company lost six flag bearers. Stephen grabbed up the flag and held it throughout the rest of the fight. For his gallantry he suffered a bullet wound through his cheek. While his wound was being dressed a colleague remarked: "The Damn Yankees tipped you, did they?" From that moment on, he became "Tip" Marks and kept the name all of his life.

A Glimpse of Loneliness
A Letter From The Field
By William Burton Lance

William Burton Lance penned a letter to his father and mother while camped near Murfreesboro, Tennessee. He was serving in the 60th Regiment of the North Carolina Volunteers. It was October 22, 1862, just eight or nine weeks before the terrible battle of Murfreesboro.

My dear father and mother:

I seat myself this evening to drop you a few lines which leave me only tolerable well. I have a bad cold and have had now for two or three days but I hope it will soon wear off. I sincerely hope these few lines will reach you and find you all enjoying good health and doing well. I have nothing very interesting to write to you any more than we had orders to cook two days "rashings," to march down to Nashville, but while we were cooking, the order was countermanded. So we don't know when we will have to leave here. We stand in readiness every day looking for orders.

There was a bad accident in our Regiment yesterday evening. There was some of our men cleaning some guns. One man that belonged to Reynolds Company was cleaning his gun and went to hand another man a piece of sandpaper and his gun fired. It shot one man by the name of Eliga Night. It killed him instantly. The ball went through his neck just below the ear and the ball struck another man in the shoulder and lodged somewhere in him. The doctor says it is a doubtful case whether he gets over it or not. They are going to bury Night now while I am writing. The health of our Regiment is tolerable good only we have plenty of mumps here at this time.

Dear father, I would like to see you all very much, but I can't at present and I fear I never will see your faces any more in this life, but I hope that we all will be prepared to meet in a better world than this where there is no more war — no parting of friends. You have no idea how bad I feel when I think of home, when I think of my little children that I once had the opportunity of being with and the pleasure that I have had with them. It nearly breaks my heart when I think of them but I will try and put it off the best I can. Tell Delia I would like to be at home with her, to help her take care of the children. I would much rather be at home than here where we have to lay and sleep on the cold camp ground. When we leave here, we will have to leave our tent and take the weather as it comes. I want you to ask John Presley if he will cut wood for Delia for what he owes me.

I will close for the present, hoping to hear from you soon. Direct your letter to Murfreesboro, Tennessee, 60th Regiment, North Carolina Troop, in care of Captain Fletcher.

I remain you son.
W. B. Lance

William survived the battle of Murfreesboro where 12,000 troops from either side were killed or wounded. He was eventually captured by the Federals and died at Camp Douglas, Illinois, a union prison, on January 8, 1864. He was directly related to Lance of modern day Lance Cracker fame.

A Strong Willed Woman
Provided by Pender R. McElroy

Henry Correll, son of plantation owners Christian and Sarah Correll, fell in love with Polly McLean and married her. She lived near Salisbury in Rowan county, North Carolina and Henry lived down the road near China Grove. Polly was a petite beauty standing barely five feet tall, but she had some mighty large convictions. She was totally against slavery in any form and persuaded Henry to leave the plantation and move to Little Pine Creek in the remote mountains of western North Carolina. Their farm was in Madison County where slavery was practically non-existent. Henry and Polly belonged to the Whigs, an anti-slavery political party. When the Republican Party replaced the Whigs, they quickly joined. As mountain people, they led a simple, self-sufficient life of farming and gardening, a far cry from the plantation life Henry had known as a child. By the time the war began, Henry and Polly had ten children and Henry was forty-one years old. Nevertheless he volunteered his services and became a private in the Union army.

About midway through the war, Henry was badly injured when he fell from a horse. He was placed in a Union army hospital near the Cumberland Gap in Kentucky, well more than a hundred miles from Polly and his children back at Little Pine Creek. When Polly received word about Henry's serious condition, she gathered her children, packed provisions on a horse, and began the long walk across the mountains of western North Carolina and eastern Tennessee. Alone with the children of various ages, Polly lead the way through the mountains which had few roads and homesteads were scarce. Occasionally they were given provisions by a kindly farmer and allowed to sleep in a barn. At other times they slept where they stopped at the end of the day. Along the way they had to contend with Union troops, Confederate troops, and worst of all, bushwhackers, outlaws who held no allegiance to any country, but merely robbed and preyed on the weak. By a conservative estimate the trip must have taken five or six weeks.

Against overwhelming odds, Polly and her children made it to the Union hospital and set up camp outside the compound. With Polly's daily nursing, Henry finally regained enough strength to leave the hospital. He was mustered out of the army and walked home with Polly and his children. In November, 1865 Polly had an eleventh child, named Henry Jr. Both Henry and Polly lived into old age, Republicans to the end.

A Family Coincidence
Provided by Michael Andrews

Shortly after the beginning of the War Between the States, Confederate officials determined to build the world's first ironclad ship. With this impenetrable vessel, the Confederates could eliminate the coastal blockade imposed upon them by the larger Union navy. To this end the Southerners raised a frigate, the *Merrimac*, scuttled by Union troops as they abandoned the U.S. navy yard at Norfolk, Virginia. They commissioned a designer and commenced the work.

Meanwhile, Northern authorities learned about the *Merrimac* and hastily planned the construction of an ironclad of their own. The construction of these war-ships was nothing less than a frantic race to the finish. Remarkably, the *Merrimac*, re-christened the CSS *Virginia*, was put into service on February 17, 1862 and the Union ironclad, the *Monitor*, was finished on February twenty-fifth, just eight days later. Both ships sailed directly to a strategic port at Hampton Roads, Virginia. The *Virginia* reached the destination just a few hours before the *Monitor*. But a few hours was enough for the *Virginia*, with her protective siding and eleven large guns, to sink the Union's USS *Cumberland*, which had 32 guns, and the USS *Congress*, which had 52 guns. They also succeeded in chasing the USS *Minnesota* aground before retiring for the evening.

The crew of the *Virginia* was surprised the next morning to see that the *Monitor* had arrived. These two impregnable war machines pounded each other for over four hours with little effect. The cannon balls bounced off the sloped sides of the two-inch iron plates. The invention of the ironclad ushered in a new era of ship building and naval warfare. Little did anyone know that without one family, neither of these historically famous ships might have been built in 1862.

It seems the iron works at Buffalo Gap, Virginia was busy making cannon balls in 1861 as was the De La Mater Iron Works in New York. The Forrer brothers, Daniel and Henry

Tony Zeiss

owned the Virginia iron works. The De La Mater family of New York owned the De La Mater iron works. When the call came in for iron plating to cover the *Virginia* and the *Monitor*, both families got busy filling the order. By an interesting twist of fate, the son in law of Charles Forrer, grandson of Daniel Forrer, was Robert De La Mater from the owners of the New York foundry. A family coincidence to say the least!

Homesick Horse
Provided by Marjorie Short

Marjorie Short's great grandfather, David Goodman Crews, was only twenty-two years old when he joined Company A of the 44th North Carolina Regiment. In the Confederate army it was sometimes customary to allow new recruits to bring their own horses. David and his horse "Skipper" entered the service of their country together, leaving their beloved home in Granville County, North Carolina. David and Skipper saw plenty of action in the eastern theatre and David was promoted to sergeant.

At the terrible battle of Chancellorsville, May first and second of 1863, David was wounded in the shoulder. He recovered from his wounds and continued serving the war effort with the faithful Skipper by his side. It is difficult to determine if David and "Skipper" were able to visit their home during his long military service, but it is safe to assume David often thought of the homeplace. As events were to unfold, Skipper must have also reminisced about his home.

David, like most young men who fought on either side, became weary, but hardened to the rigors of the elements, poor diet, and the battlefield. He must have thought it to be a particularly bad piece of luck when he was knocked off his horse by another Minie ball in the same shoulder that was wounded at Chancellorsville. It was even worse luck because he was shot near Appomatox Court House in April, 1865 just a day or two before Confederate General Robert E. Lee surrendered to General Ulysses Grant. But worst of all, he and Skipper were separated and neither knew where the other was. David was taken to a makeshift hospital and lost all track of Skipper.

After several weeks of convalescence, David, like all his fellow soldiers, eagerly began walking the hundred miles or so back to Granville County, North Carolina. In the meantime "Skipper" had already made his way back to the homeplace, a full two weeks ahead of David! A house servant saw "Skipper" first and ran into the house to tell David's father. "Skipper's home! Skipper's home! She shouted.

"How do you know its Skipper?" he asked.

"Because when I spit at him, he kicked me!" she replied.

How Skipper found his way home gives cause for speculation until this day. We can only surmise he determined to return home to look for David or he was homesick like all the troops. You can only imagine the joyful reunion between David and his pal Skipper. David lived a long life and died with two Minie balls still in his shoulder.

Mama Stayed Angry Till She Died
Provided by Chuck Northcutt

Mr. Northcutt's grandmother, Ada Iola Childress, told this story about her father and mother who had to endure the humiliation of having the hated Union General William Tecumseh Sherman occupy their home as a headquarters.

It was on September 1, 1864 that General Sherman's troops occupied Atlanta, Georgia. The citizens of Atlanta where frightened and bewildered after the long campaign against them and they were shocked by the reality that all was probably lost. Among them were Dr. William Childress and his wife who lived in a large home on Peach Tree Street in the Cross Keys area. The structure caught Sherman's eye and he commandeered it as his headquarters. Upon discovering that Dr. Childress was a medical doctor, Sherman pressed him into immediate service.

Dr. Childress was taken to the railroad freight yard which had become the place for all the wounded soldiers from both armies. There was no medicine, very few bandages, and the sanitary conditions were terrible. Dr. Childress converted a baggage room in the train depot into a makeshift operating room. Here he amputated the limbs of scores of boys and men as the only means to stop the deadly spread of gangrene. Every minute counted and Dr. Childress worked non-stop for several days. His helpers threw the severed limbs out the window onto large baggage carts to be hauled away. By the time he returned to his wife on Peach Tree Street, she hardly recognized him. He had lost considerable weight, was splattered with blood, and looked like walking death.

Dr. Childress recovered and lived until 1923. He and realized their beautiful home, now a National Historic Landmark, was spared only because Sherman took it for his headquarters. Nonetheless, Mrs. Childress got angry every time she thought about the occupation of her home by Sherman. And she had one visible reminder she often pointed out to visitors and family.

It seems iron was becoming a very scarce commodity toward the end of the war. Cannons are useless without cannon balls. Sherman ordered his men to confiscate all the iron they could find to be melted into armaments. Unfortunately the Childress house had a large iron kettle hanging on a swiveling hook by their fireplace. This iron hook was fastened to the side of the fireplace mantel. The union troops took the kettle and ripped the hook out of the mantel leaving a deep scare that can be seen to this day. "They never would fix it!" Ada Iola's Mother would tell her daughter. "And mama stayed mad about it until she died," reported Ada Iola.

Brotherly Love
As told by Larry Walker

My great grandfather, Joseph King, was only thirteen years old when the War Between the States broke out. His four older brothers quickly joined the third North Carolina Regiment and went off toward Virginia. Although he was too young to become a soldier, Joe resolved to assist the Confederate cause in any way possible. He lived in Wilmington, North Carolina just a few miles north of Fort Fisher. This earthen fort was strategically located at the entrance of a critical Southern port that was being hastily constructed near the mouth of the Cape Fear River. As long as this fort could be defended, the port could be held open for blockade-runners to continue importing supplies to the Confederacy and exporting cotton to foreign markets. Fort Fisher was a constant problem for the Union Navy, which was supposed to block all sea traffic from getting into or leaving southern ports.

Keeping the soldiers at Fort Fisher fed was a problem for Colonel William Lamb, a former lawyer and newspaper editor, who was charged with strengthening the defenses and protecting the mouth of the river. Hearing about the colonel's need for provisions, Joe's employer, Mr. Thomas Johnson, built a slaughter pen near the fort. Joe's job, besides helping to butcher, was to drive cattle from Wilmington area farms to Fort Fisher. Of course, Joe drove the cattle on foot, sometimes from more than twenty miles away. He did so on a regular basis until yellow fever broke out in Wilmington. Colonel Lamb then banned all contact from Wilmington, fearing his troops might catch the dreaded disease.

Unfortunately, Joe, like nearly everyone else in Wilmington, came down with the illness. Six hundred and fifty people of the town's 3,000 inhabitants died. Joe was near death when one of his older brother, Isaac, himself recently wounded at the terrible battle of Malvern Hill, traveled to Wilmington to help.

This dedicated brother took Joe out of Wilmington and back to a farm near Myrtle Grove Sound where both recuperated. Joe's mother fed him a glass containing one teaspoon of pulverized sulfur, the yolk of one egg, and about a wineglass full of new corn whiskey each day for nine days.

Joe continued serving the people of his region by founding a church and preaching for fifty-six years. He died in 1948 at the age of 99 years and six months. It is doubtful he ever thirsted for whiskey after his mother's yellow fever cure.

Grandma's Missing!
As Told by Anne Barrett Macomson Rivers and Compiled by Robert E. Macomson

Eighteen-year-old Lucy Walton Barrett grew up on a plantation near Jackson, Mississippi destined to lead the life of a Southern Belle until War erupted and changed her life forever. Her affluent father sided with the Confederacy and converted all of his wealth into Confederate currency, which became worthless after the war. Lucy carried away many memories of that awful time when their plantation was alternatively occupied by both armies. On one occasion the whole family was distressed to find Grandma was missing. It happened this way.

It was probably in the spring of 1863 when Lucy and her family, all women and children since the men were all enlisted, were warned by a Union messenger to leave the house. The Union forces expected to begin a battle the next morning at daylight and the Union commander was afraid their house might be caught in the crossfire of the opposing armies. One of the youngsters of the family knew of a dry creek bed with high banks that would help protect them when the firing began. They loaded food, bedclothes, and other necessities into a wagon, including grandma who was most reluctant to go.

After traveling a good distance, the women and children arrived at their destination just before dark. They distributed the blankets and pillows and settled in for the night. Grandma fussed and fumed and complained she should be allowed to sleep in her own bed, Yankees or not. After much coaxing, grandma finally settled down and got quiet. In spite of the discomfort, the family drifted off to sleep.

Morning broke with cannon fire shaking the ground and frightening everyone awake. Much to everyone's dismay grandma was missing! The battle continued until noon and Lucy and her family worried a great deal about grandma. They could envision her lost or killed in the conflagration of the battle.

When the sounds of the battle ceased, they hurried home as fast as possible. They needn't have worried about grandma. They found her asleep in her own bed!

Lucy used to remark: "Nobody ever knew how she managed to find her way back to the house in the dark or how she slept through the morning's battle, but she did!"

Two Brothers And A Ghost
As Told by Tony Crumbley about His Great-Great Grandfather Joe Pinion

Benjamin and Jane Pinion had eight children born between 1839 and 1867. Four were boys old enough to join the fighting during the War. Two of these sons, Thomas W. and Joe Darling Pinion joined Company B of the Fifth North Carolina Regiment on August 8, 1862. Colonel William J. Hill commanded the regiment which was assigned to D. H. Hill's division.

Twenty days after the Pinion boy's enlistment, the entire division moved to join the army of Northern Virginia. They crossed into Maryland on September fourth and fifth. On September tenth, their division moved out from Fredrick, Maryland as a rear guard for General Longstreet's column. Over the next several days the Pinion brothers fought in many skirmishes and battles. During this campaign, hundreds of men in Thomas and Joe's brigade lost their lives or were wounded. In addition, 187 men were missing; many who simply tired of the war and walked home.

On October 25, 1862 Thomas and Joe deserted the army. Thomas was caught and arrested for desertion in March the next year, but escaped on May 9, 1863. Thomas was later given a federal parole in Charlotte, North Carolina after the war ended.

Joe's circumstances, however, followed a unique path. The official Confederate records indicated he was killed in action (one day after his desertion) and placed on the roll of honor.

Other reports say Joe escaped to Tennessee where he joined the Union army, trading his gray uniform for a blue one. At the end of the war, Joe returned to North Carolina, married, and had thirteen children. Whether it was his ghost or the real Joe, Tony Crumbley says it was lucky for him because one of Joe's children became his great grandmother. Joe Pinion was officially buried on September 15, 1918 and has not been seen since!

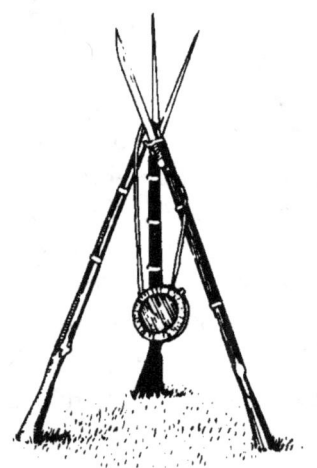

Kindness Prevailed
Provided by Richard F. Green

Jimmie Moring, Great Uncle of Richard Green, benefited from the goodness of people while fighting for his country during a time when kindness appeared to be in short supply.

Jimmie's North Carolina regiment, like so many others, moved up and down Virginia's Shenandoah Valley fighting battle after battle. In one of these, he was badly wounded in the leg and left on the battlefield for dead. After dark that evening, Jimmie saw enemy troops plundering whatever they could from fallen soldiers. Fearing execution should these soldiers find him, Jimmie began crawling toward dense cover. After several hours, he saw a lighted window of a farmhouse and determined to reach it.

That house turned out to belong to an angel of mercy named P. W. Leomior. She and her family took Jimmie into their home and tended him for a full year before he was fit to travel back to North Carolina. Jimmie was grateful he was not put under the care of army surgeons, amputations were the rule of the day, and he was pleased the enemy did not find him on the battlefield. But he was most appreciative of Mrs. Leomior and her family for saving his life. In fact, he corresponded with them many times after the war and they remained life-long friends. The following exerts from one of Mrs. Leomior's letters, dated March 28, 1866, provides some poignant insight into her kind spirit.

Dear Jimmie,

I have received your letter of the 18th and am very glad to learn that you are all well and that your leg has improved much. I had not supposed you would be able to travel without your crutch and am really very glad that you are able to get along without it. You ought to be very thankful that you are as well off as you are, with your life spared and your health and strength much returned.

You say you have written to me several times, but I do not think I have received more than one letter since the war. I ought to have answered that one, but we have had so much confusion in the country and sickness in our family that I neglected to do so. We had troops stationed here all last summer and fall, but there are none here now. We have only an agent of the government, a tax collector. We have had a good deal of sickness. Alice had typhoid fever last summer and money is very scarce. Many of our people have been ruined by the war; being deprived of nearly all their property except their land. This means they will not be able to pay their debts (and taxes). But we must all trust in the Lord for help and do the best we can. We were too ungrateful for the many blessings we enjoyed before the war. What seems to us an affliction, may be intended for our good.

I have no news that would interest you. I would like very much to see you and if I had money a plenty, I think I would pay you a visit. As to the little that we did for you when you were wounded, it was no more than our duty, and we were glad we were able to make you a little more comfortable, perhaps, than you would have been in a hospital with strangers. We are commanded to do all we can for the sick and the afflicted, and we should never neglect to do so when it is in our power.

Very Truly, your friend

P. W. Leomior

Nothing Was Safe
Provided by Robert E. Macomson

Lucy Walton Barrett, the eighteen-year-old daughter of a wealthy Mississippi planter saw the ugliness of war when Federal soldiers plundered their house time after time during those dark days of the war. Two such occasions reflect clear images of what citizens all over the South and parts of the north endured when opposing troops came through their land.

As usual, the Barrett family received little notice the Yankees were on the march in their part of the county. The house servants didn't even have time to bury the silverware in the woods. Instead, they placed the precious silver pieces on top of a large wardrobe which had a pediment high enough to hide them from sight. After searching the house and confiscating little, the Yankees spied the large wardrobe. Thinking it was hiding a door to another room, several of the soldiers heaved the piece of furniture to the side. In doing so, the silverware rolled around and clattered like broken glass. The soldiers quickly discovered the loot and took every piece with them.

On another occasion, foraging soldiers, a fancy name for thieves, entered the Barrett home searching for food and valuables. With the silverware gone, the last remaining thing of particular value was a bolt of beautiful French silk material. Lucy's father had purchased it from French merchant seamen. The ladies were hoping to prepare social dresses from the treasured cloth.

Unfortunately, their hopes were diminished and their anger increased when the pilfering troops found the cloth. Their last memory of this luxury item was of a Yankee's bayonet stuck through the bolt of silk with yards of it streaming out behind him as he left.

Editor's note: Lucy always maintained the soldier did not take the cloth as loot. "It was purely and act of destruction and meanness."

The Survivor
Provided by Sam Kipp

Seventeen-year-old George Rexford sneaked from his log cabin home in Gaines Township, Pennsylvania to join the army. He was reluctant to leave his three brothers and two sisters, but President Lincoln had called for volunteers to preserve the Union and George didn't want to miss the action. He made it into an infantry unit only to be recalled when his mother told Army officials he was under age. After turning eighteen, George unsuccessfully pleaded with his mother to let him fight the Confederates. Finally, on February 22, 1864 he again ran away from home and joined the army. This time he was of age and enlisted in Company F of the 45th Pennsylvania Regiment.

George didn't have long to wait for action. He was a participant in the deadly and weary cat and mouse shuffling between Union general U.S. Grant and the Confederate commander, Robert E. Lee. Both armies were constantly repositioning, moving ever closer toward Richmond, the Confederate capital. By the end of May 1864 Grant moved his army toward Cold Harbor, a dusty crossroads just north of Richmond. The Union general ordered an attack for June 2nd, but high command blunders forced a postponement until the next day, giving General Lee's Troops time to dig in. Grant's troops, including George Rexford, charged the entrenched confederates on the morning of June 3rd across an open field of about five acres. The result was disastrous. Seven thousand federal troops fell in less than half an hour. It is believed that this short, decisive battle still holds the record for the most casualties in the shortest time period for American soldiers.

George was wounded, but unlike most of his colleagues, survived. He was discharged in the middle of July after recovering, but he lost one of his legs. Unfortunately, George was not able to wear an artificial limb because of some complications with gangrene, but he handled crutches very well. In fact, he handled them well enough to travel to Ford's Theater in Washington City. By coincidence, he attended the theater on the same night, April 14, 1865, that John Wilkes Booth assassinated President Lincoln.

George settled down in Germania, Pennsylvania, marrying Elizabeth Cooper. They had five children, four of whom died of diphtheria within days of each other. George's surviving son died in a tragic saw mill accident some time later, then his wife of some fifty years passed away. After a time, all of George's brothers and sisters also passed leaving George as the surviving person of his generation. This remarkable man held tenaciously to life and finally died in 1935 at the fine age of ninety-one. His obituary noted that he was one of the last surviving Civil War veterans in Pennsylvania and was the last surviving veteran from his township.

Execution Of A Deserter
From the Diary of A. Crawford Gwin

Crawford Gwin was a member of Company F of the Pennsylvania Seventy-six volunteers, also known as the Keystone Zouaves. Gwin's company was mustered into the Union army in 1861 and was ordered to serve along the eastern coast. While stationed at Hilton Head Island, South Carolina, Gwin witnessed the execution of a deserter. The narrative in private Gwin's own words provides a vivid picture of the harsh discipline which was often applied during the War Between the States.

Monday, 1st of December, 1862

Warm and cloudy this morning. As this was the day for the execution of a man of the 9th Maine Regiment who was named and tried for desertion at Florida in June last. He was sentenced to be shot in presence of this command. Early in the morning, preparations were made and all the regiments marched outside of the breast-works and formed in a hollow square opened at one side. At 11am the hearse made its appearance escorted by fifty of the 47th New York Volunteers commanded by Major VanBurst, Provost Marshall of this place. The prisoner was seated in the hearse when they arrived in the center of the square.

The prisoner got out of the wagon and walked to the place where he was to be shot. He was guarded by two of the poll bearers. Without arms, a coffin was then taken to him and he sat down on it. Charges of his trial were read to him. He then stood and spoke as follows: "Fellow soldiers, I want you to take warning by my words and seek salvation of the Lord before it is too late. I am not guilty of the crime for which I have been condemned to death." The following lines he handed to the printer:

"I am about to suffer death which punishment I am willing to bear for a warning to others which may be led astray by bad company. Fellow soldiers, you should take warning by me and keep off bad company and shun everything that is bad. Keep good company and you will be respected by your worst enemies. Oh may God bless the officers of the Forty-seventh New York Regiment. They have done everything within their powers and they brought me back to religion and religious papers that led me on the right road to my savior. Oh! May God help and sustain them throughout the peril of the battles that they may come out victorious in them all and may God speed the time when peace shall once more be, and the friends that are here at war will be going home to their families." — Albert W. Lunt

The prisoner was ordered to take his position behind the coffin, kneeling on the coffin in a half-stooped position. The Provost Marshall tied a white handkerchief around his head. Two preachers then went to him and had prayer, one on either side. The preachers went away and twelve soldiers, who were standing in line about twelve paces in front of him, took aim and at twenty-eight minutes past eleven o'clock, the guns went off and he fell forward over his coffin, struck by all the balls of which pronounced him fatal. He did not move a limb after falling. He was dead in two minutes. His body was put into the coffin which was put in the wagon and took back near the graveyard. No persons went along but the pallbearers.

So ended the life of a traitor. No honor was due him. This should be a warning to all soldiers never to betray their trust or to desert to the enemy. For desertion in time of war is always punished by death. We returned to camp hoping we had all learned a lesson we never should forget.

Henry's Letter
Featured by the *Charlotte News*, June 11, 1964

Mrs. Bob Sutton of Charlotte, North Carolina discovered this letter from a Yankee soldier to his sister and sent it to the *Charlotte News*. She commented: "This letter, written in 1863, proves beyond a doubt that while we endeavor to change human nature, it has the disconcerting habit of remaining static. Loneliness of the soldier during war has not abated over the centuries."

We don't know who Henry was or exactly where he came from, but his letter is very typical of those written by hundreds of thousands of young men who slept on the ground, ate poor food, and fought boredom, ravaging insects, sickness, fatigue, and each other. Mostly, though, they dreamed of home and those they loved so dearly.

"My Dear Sister, Baton Rouge, La. July 18, 1863
I came up here last night from Donaldsonville for a little rest. Have been with the boys since the 28th of May and during this time on duty all of the while and partly alone. The camp is established here and it almost seems like home.

We had a fight at Donaldsonville the 13th. Advanced too hastily on the Rebs ere our forces had arrived from Port Hudson. In consequence were driven back, some 20 killed and missing out of our regiment. Retreated back to the river under cover of the gunboats where no Reb dared to come.

The Mississippi River is once more clear and boats began to come down from above. Should not be surprised if we returned home by way of the Mississippi instead of sea. Hope that may be the case.

I received Laura's letter yesterday. Was glad to get it. It did some good to read it. At the late fight at Donaldsonville, Payson Nash was taken prisoner by the enemy and later paroled. Some 15 from our regiment were captured and paroled. While with the Rebs, they received nothing but a pint of corn meal a day. Poor living rather.

Our Colonel W. L. Bartlett returned home yesterday. Quite a number of the sick and wounded also returned. Know not how many days must elapse before we start. Preparations are in the making for our departure. I keep my place and have had a lieutenancy offered to me in a regiment. Refused it as I wish to come home.

All the Cheshin people are well. Heard today that Washington is captured by Lee. Can hardly believe this. Also heard that 'Old Abe' is dead. Street farces which I do not believe.

Write to me. I direct this to Cheshin, thinking your school must be out by now.

Your affectionate brother, Henry"

Love's A Powerful Motivator
As told by Robert L. Taylor
August, 1995

Sometime in the year of 1862, fifteen year old Lucius Taylor, a farm boy from just outside Grand Rapids, Michigan succeeded in joining the U.S. Army. He was under age. Two of his older brothers, George and Walter had also attempted to join under age when the war broke out in 1860, but failed. Nevertheless they both reached the eligible age of eighteen by 1862 and became legitimate members of Michigan outfits. All three brothers were then sent South to fight for the Union. Young Lucius, later to become the great uncle of Robert L. Taylor, was thought to be too small to carry a rifle and was assigned to drive a supply wagon for the Sixth Michigan Infantry of the Army of the Republic.

During the spring of 1863, Lucius and his brothers were camped near the Big Black River next to the small village of Oak Ridge just fifteen miles east of Vicksburg, Mississippi. General U. S. Grant was positioning his army to make an invasion upon this last strategic confederate stronghold in the western theatre of the war. During this pre-attack stage of the Vicksburg campaign, rifle skirmishing was a regular occurrence all along the lines. Pickets were posted at all times.

After one small skirmish, Lucius discovered a young Confederate soldier lying in the woods seriously wounded. Having compassion for the boy, Lucius tended to him and was persuaded to help get him to his home a few miles away. The young Confederate was about the same age as Lucius and carried the last name of Fears. Lucius carried the soldier on his back nearly all the way home through enemy territory.

The Fears family expressed much gratitude to Lucius and showed him exceptional hospitality, except for one sister, Ella. This beautiful teenager made it clear that even though Lucius had saved her brother's life; she would have nothing to do with a Yankee.

Lucius, however, was absolutely star struck by Ella. In fact, he lingered around the Fear home for several days, but try as he might, the object of his attentions wouldn't give him the time of day. Hour after hour, Lucius fell deeper in love with Ella Fears. He finally decided that his love for Ella was stronger than his allegiance to the Grand Army of the Republic. In short order he traded in his blue uniform for a gray one. He ended up fighting against his former friends and brothers, but it must have been worth it all to Lucius. Ella had a quick change of heart and they married soon after the war.

Lucius and Ella settled near Mechanicsburg, Mississippi and raised eight children. Lucius lived until 1914 and never regretted following the passion of his heart.

Eye Witness At Gettysburg
Excerpts from the July 1, 1963 issue of the *Charlotte News*

July 1, 1863 found the famed Eleventh North Carolina Regiment poised to see battle in the rolling hills just south and west of Gettysburg, Pennsylvania. Young Billie Taylor, from Charlotte, North Carolina clutched his heavy rifle in anticipation of the order to open fire. As accustomed to fighting as he was, each new battle created its own fear. This was no exception. Billie's own description, in a letter to his mother, provides a realistic picture of that momentous occasion.

Billie and his company were engaged on the first day of the battle at Gettysburg when a volley sounded overhead accompanied by the whizzing sound which precedes death, and a grape shot, the size of an egg, struck Major Ross in his right side. "It went right through him. He lived about four hours and we buried him in our company. I got a piece of plank and put his name on it with his rank, for a head-board."

Meanwhile, Billie's regiment was moved into the breach of the battle. According to Billie, dozens of men fainted from the heat alone as the attack began. Billowing clouds of black smoke rose from the surrounding fields as General Lee's Army of Northern Virginia clashed with General Mead's Army of the Potomac. Nearly 200,000 men and boys were fighting for an important victory, fighting for their lives.

"You ought to have seen our brigade when it charged," Billie wrote. "It was through an old open field and it was at an awful cost, but we paid it to them two-fold. The Iron Brigade Yankees tried to stand, but it was no use. We stood within twenty yards of each other for about fifteen minutes. They finally had to give way, and when they did, we just mowed them down."

At day's end, row after row of sun-baked corpses lay at the mercy of predators. "We held possession of the field the first and second days and a part of the field the third day. Our company went into the fight again on the third day with thirty men

General James Johnston Pettigrew

out of more than a hundred who participated in the first day's fighting. We were not engaged the second day, but could see the battle raging from where we stood. Our company came out of the third day with eight men and myself. I was hit by grapeshot, but it did no damage. Oh, my sock leg was shot through and my sword scabbard was struck, so you can just imagine how thick the balls were."

The next day, General Lee began his retreat across the Potomac, but General Meade, inexplicably failed to follow. A Union cavalry unit did follow, however. Billie describes what happened. "We were lying down asleep when the enemy's cavalry, a battalion of them, charged in among us. They killed our General Pettigrew there. They thought we were stragglers, but they were sadly mistaken. We killed, wounded, or captured the whole of them. But it was hard for our General Pettigrew to be killed by some rascally cavalry when he had gone all the way through Gettysburg.

A parting example of dedication and optimism was exhibited in Billie's letter. "They claim a victory at Gettysburg, but if they whipped, why not follow us? We waited for them. If we do fight here, we will give them one of the worst thrashings they ever got."

The Money Dress
Provided by Dr. Ted Gasper

D r. Gasper's brave ancestor wrote this account of one of her experiences as a young woman in South Carolina during Union General Sherman's devastating march through that country. In November 1864 O. P. (Mary) Bouknight married Christie Poppenheim, a young Confederate soldier who had been wounded at the battle of Sharpsburg (Antietam) in September, 1862 and was now assigned to lighter duty at Charleston, South Carolina. They lived at her father's plantation, "Gallant Hill," some twenty miles outside of town. Mary's words aptly describe her world during the first few months of her marriage.

"The whole country was in a most unsettled condition, and we became reconciled to the war continuing this way for ten years or longer. One day we had a report of a victory; the next day a report of disaster to our scantily clothed and poorly fed soldiers. Prisoners were often carried by the plantation gates and my mother was often terrified at the thought of some of them escaping and entering the house.

When Christie went to work at the quartermaster's in Charleston, we would busy ourselves sewing for the soldiers, helping to make Confederate coffee from potatoes cut into little squares, dried, then parched and ground. We also made confederate candles of myrtle wax.

One afternoon Christie came in with a look of anxious distress and told me to pack my trunks and be ready to leave by the next train. Sherman was marching through Georgia and South Carolina would soon be invaded. Charleston was to be evacuated. Sherman had threatened to lay the city in ashes and sow it in salt. We must leave to my grandfather Bouknight's plantation on the Saluda River, fifty miles above Columbia."

Mary and Christie and four servants hurried to the train station and began a confusing trip Northwest toward Columbia only to witness the glowing fires of that capital city. Sherman had gotten there before them. Mary and her husband were transporting more than their clothes and jewelry; Mary had most of the family fortune sewed into the lining of her flowing dress…one hundred thousand dollars! This seemed the safest place for the money to be hidden since the Yankees would surely search everything and everyone except Mrs. Poppenheim. One hundred thousand dollars in those days would be worth fifty times that amount today.

After many different trains and coaches, the family and a few companions, including Mr. William Steinmyer and Captain Atkinson, traveled across the northern part of the state toward her father's plantation. They got as far as Liberty Hill and put up at a plantation owned by Mr. John Brown. By now Confederates were retreating from Columbia and the Yankees were in pursuit all over the country, making it too dangerous for travel. On the next day, the first of several regiments of Yankees pillaged the Brown plantation. Mary described it this way:

"In a few minutes a band of ruffians, a wild, savage looking set, rushed in the house and swept all the silverware from the table, ran upstairs, broke open doors and all the locked drawers. The utmost confusion prevailed. The hammering sounded like one dozen carpenters were at work. Soon all the floors were covered with scattered papers as they searched for money and valuables. I asked for protection from their commanding officer, which he promises. Christie and I go upstairs and find my trunks broken open and everything scattered over the floor. They took my jewelry and the four thousand dollars we had in a trunk. Oh! What a scene; impossible to describe. Money, jewelry, and clothing of every description was taken by those demons!"

This terrible scene is repeated many times until the first of March when Sherman's troops finally leave the region. In the end, the invaders burned every building on the Brown plantation except the house. One of her most fearful memories occurred when the Yankees interrogate Christie in an upstairs room, trying to prove that he is an active enemy so they can kill him or at least take him prisoner.

"I fear he is up with them too long. I fear foul play and determined to go up stairs. My knees tremble at every step because I'm afraid they will hear the bumps made by the sound of the money sewed up in the lining of my dress. When I reached the top of the stairs, the sharp little captain had Christie. Christie said, 'Mary, this man thinks I am a captain in the Rebel army and wants to take me prisoner.' I had to swear that he was not and that we had been married a very short time and were on our way to my father's plantation. Then I gave him the Masonic sign of distress (which my brother gave me before going to war). The captain looked down, shut his mouth tight, then said, 'go on.' And we lost no time in going. When this party came downstairs they captured Mr. Atkinson and Mr. Steinmyer and took them off to their camp. How we pitied their fate.

The Yankees were pushing rapidly for Camden to plunder and rob the peaceful, quiet little town. We are starving here, having nothing left to eat but sorghum molasses and black short bread. Sherman's army has left no living thing on their route; nothing but blackened chimneys and smoking ruins mark his path from Columbia to here. Pillage, robbery, fire, and ruin marked their footsteps here. A sigh of relief and a prayer of thankfulness that our lives were sparred was breathed as we saw the last Yankee soldier disappear from the devastated little village."

Post Note: The family fortune was saved.

Surprise Pillow
Provided by Clarence Kuester

Norman L. Shaw, Captain of Company D, 17th North Carolina Regiment of the Army of Northern Virginia and maternal grandfather of Clarence Kuester told a remarkable tale in a letter to his family. It was during the second battle of Cold Harbor, Virginia that Captain Shaw had one of the most unusual experiences of his military career. Entrenched Confederates defended charge after charge by General Grant's Union troops on June 2nd and 3rd of 1864. Grant's army suffered 7,000 casualties on the first day. Grant's brave soldiers, knowing the odds against assaulting an enemy well dug in, pinned their names and home addresses to their shirts so they could be identified in the event of their demise. This was the beginning of the idea of issuing identification or "dog tags" of today's modern armies. After the first day's battle, both armies dug trenches to hide in and the troops talked to each other and traded supplies during the night. Captain Shaw explains in his letter:

"Our line of breastworks was miles long, the enemy's equally long, and the two were only a few hundred yards in front. Near the center, the lines were so close that conversation could be heard even in a low tone of voice. Two men occupied each rifle pit. Quite often during the late silent hours of the night a certain signal, a whistle or a groan, would be given to announce that an exchange of presents. The Johnnies giving tobacco in exchange for coffee."

The next part of Captain Shaw's letter must have shocked his family as much as anything he had ever described about his wartime experiences.

"For some weeks both of my lieutenants had been sick in the hospital which required me to be constantly on duty night and day. With little sleep or rest, the strenuous work came very near proving serious. At last, one of my lieutenants reported for duty about dark, on a very rainy, disagreeable evening. I immediately put him in charge and after full instructions told him I was going a few feet to the rear to have a night's rest and sleep. I warned him under no conditions to disturb me unless the enemy should advance or we received orders to move. Taking my blanket, I groped my way in the dark. No lights, not even the striking of a match was allowed. I spread my blanket on the wet ground. I never could sleep sound without my head being slightly elevated so I felt around me, hoping to find a rock or billet of wood for a pillow. I was successful in finding what I thought was a large rock and laid my weary head on its hard surface. I slept soundly until the first dawn of the day.

"On arising and taking up my blanket, to my surprise and wonder, I found the pillow was neither a rock nor a piece of wood, but the skull of some unknown person who doubtless had been killed at the first battle of Cold Harbor, (June 27, 1862). His bones, after two years were exposed. Taking the skull in my hands I thus addressed the stranger: 'I don't know who you were while in the flesh, whether friend or foe, but I do know that you have proven to be a great comfort to me during the night and I claim you as a friend. I trust your soul is at rest and in token of appreciation of the pleasure your earthly remains have voluntarily and with silent consent, added to my comfort, I will now give you a decent burial.'

"Drawing my sword from its scabbard, I hurriedly dug a hole deep and large enough to hold what was once the active, intelligent, thinking member of the body. I silently and sacredly placed it in the new grave saying: 'I now commit your bones to mother earth, hoping it will not be disturbed until the resurrection morn and pray that your soul is happy in the heavenly mansions.' Then covering it, in whisper I sang the *Doxology* and dismissed this very unexpected and sad, silent funeral service."

Desperation
Provided by Bob Zeiss

"Ma, I'm desperate!" cried seventeen-year old Calvin Carey. "All my friends are joining an artillery regiment down at Indianapolis and I won't meet their regulations for height and weight. What can I do?"

"You don't meet the regulations on age either, Cal. The best thing you can do is wait until you're eighteen like the law says. By then you'll most likely meet the weight and height they want."

"But Ma. I just have to go with Billy and Jimmy and them. You've got to let me go," pleaded Calvin.

This is pretty much the dialog my father remembered his grandfather Calvin used when he often told this story about his enlistment. Back in late 1863 Calvin was a slender farm boy who stood only five foot four and a half inches and weighed about 117 pounds. His eighteenth birthday was months away and his mother did not want him to join up. After much discussion, Mrs. Carey relented and agreed to give permission for Calvin to join underage. (It was often the custom for underage boys to write the number 18 on a slip of paper and put it in their shoe. When asked by the army recruiter if they were "over eighteen" they could answer in the affirmative without lying.) The army would accept boys aged seventeen if their parents signed a permission slip, as Calvin's mother or father did, but they had regulations on height, five foot five minimum, and weight, 125 pounds. Calvin still had these two obstacles to overcome if he hoped to join that new regiment with his friends. His friends planned to muster in on December fourth, just two and a half weeks away!

Calvin's mother suggested that he just might meet the minimums if he would go to bed, have very little physical activity, and eat plenty of meat, potatoes, and bananas. (How they came by bananas in the middle of winter in 1863 has always been a mystery, but Calvin said he never ate so many bananas in his life.) He took his mother's advice and kept himself in bed or on the couch for most of the next two and a half weeks. The belief was he could grow taller by relieving the compression of cartilage between all his joints and spine. Calvin was determined to reach that height and weight minimums and must have done nothing but sleep and eat because he was mustered into the Indiana seventeenth battery, light artillery on December 4, 1863.

Calvin's military records recorded he was five foot six inches tall. He had grown an inch and a half in just seventeen or eighteen days! Calvin served in his regiment under Captain Eli Lilly (later to become famous in pharmaceuticals) and mustered out with his battery on the eighth of July 1865. Calvin saw action at Harper's Ferry, Charlestown, Fisher's Hill, New Market, Maryland Heights, Halltown, and Cedar Creek. His battery was assigned to General Phillip Sheridan during the Shenandoah Valley campaign. He lived to a ripe old age.

A Southern Woman's Grit
Provided by Brad Hudson

During the War Between the States, Southern women were left to run the farm, often with little help unless they had some servants. All of the able bodied men went off to war, many never to return. The resolve of these faithful and resilient wives has been well recorded, but the story of Mrs. Rachel Pearsall of Dublin County, near Kenansville, NC, is exemplary. She was a cousin to Mrs. Hudson's mother-in-law.

Mrs. Pearsall explained her circumstances in her reminiscence letters: "When our soldiers were off, we began to prepare to make a living. The old men managed most of the affairs, and in our part of the County we got along fairly well until the Yankees began to come up and make raids on us. Then what a time we poor women had!" At first the Yankees simply liberated all the prisoners in the local jail, took every able-bodied white men as prisoners of their own, and cut all telegraph wires. Later, toward the end of the war, General Sherman's troops ravaged the county. Mrs. Pearsall prepared as best she could. She and her two children hid the silver and jewels themselves, but enlisted the aid of two faithful servants to hide the cured meat. "I had them get the largest box they could find and bury it in the garden. We had picked out the choicest sides of meat and packed the box full. The darkies said, 'Missus, de sides will do us so much mo' good dan de hams and shoulders, fur dey will do ter cook de cabbage and greens fur er long time'. We nailed up the box, covered up the hole, and planted the garden over it. When the Yankees came our vegetables were several inches high. The soldiers dug in the ground everywhere else in their wild hunt for valuables, but hey never suspected the garden."

Mrs. Pearsall managed to hide a new set of double harness by carrying it in the night to the house of her faithful black mammy, Phyllis. They stuffed it under some planks from the floor. She hid her watch, chain, and some jewels in a tin box that was wrapped in cloth and dipped in wax. This she buried in a hole in the middle of her hen house. Not everyone was faithful to Mrs. Pearsall however. "All of our servants were faithful except the cook. She declined to take part in the hiding of our things, saying she feared the Yankees. When the Yankees came again, she demanded the smokehouse key from me and gave them all the meat we had not hidden, and then emptied the pantries. The raid lasted three weeks, and the cook fed the Yankees the best she could find at my house. She cooked for them too!" Mrs. Pearsall continues: "The Yankees pillaged the house from cellar to attic, opened every drawer, closet and trunk and took what suited them. They treated my father-in-law worse than they did me. They threw my sick aunt out of her bed so they could tumble the bed upside down. They found father's best suit, which had been hidden there. All the beautiful quilts, which had been made by the older members of the family and were highly prized, were put on the old sore back mules and horses and carried off. They brought out father's nice carriage, filled it with meat, making the servants dress chickens and turkeys which they hung all around the carriage, then hitched two mules to it and drove away. They had taken the beautiful carriage horses off the previous day."

The unfaithful cook soon informed Mrs. Pearsall that she would cook no more. Mrs. Pearsall engaged another woman, "a free Negro who lived on their place," to do the cooking. This enraged the old cook who began to make threats on the lives of Mrs. Pearsall and the new cook, Matilda. Meanwhile, the townspeople of Kenansville had hired federal soldiers to guard their places and provide protection from straggling Yankees. One of these federal "guards" heard about the cook's threats and rode out to the Pearsall place to investigate. Rachel Pearsall relates: "The cook acknowledged that she had said all the things he had heard, but she didn't intend to 'burn up Miss Rachel.' I plead for her because I thought the man was going to give her a good whipping. He told me to go into the house. I tried to take her with me, but the guard ordered her to go behind the barn. Just then I heard one of my neighbors coming down the road and I ran out to the front gate and plead with him to interfere. While I was talking to him I heard a gun fire and he said, 'It's too late, he has killed her.' When he left, the servants, obeying my instructions, made a coffin, dressed her in her best clothes, and gave her a decent burial."

Fortunately, Mr. Pearsall returned from the fighting in the early summer. He enlisted the aid of their servants to farm with him as free men. They all stayed and shared in the crops and livestock as a means to begin living on their own.

Divine Intervention

From the *Benjamin Morrow Papers*
Billy Graham Center Archives

Young Benjamin Morrow Coffey probably wasn't thinking about his ancestral roots that fateful day at the battle of Gettysburg when the Eleventh North Carolina Regiment went into action. It is for sure he wasn't thinking about his grandchildren to come. However, Benny Coffey did come from a distinguished pedigree of Scots, his ancestor William Alexander was secretary of Scotland, the first Earle of Sterling and was given the territories of Nova Scotia and New Brunswick by King James the first. A later ancestor, Ezra Alexander, signed the Mecklenburg County, North Carolina Declaration of Independence from England in 1775, a full year before representatives of the original colonies signed a similar declaration. And little did he know at the time, but his grandchildren, one in particular, would influence the world. But none of this was on his mind as his regiment charged the Federals at the fateful battle of Gettysburg.

Indeed, Benny was probably thinking what most of the young men were thinking when they went into battle with cannon shot exploding above their heads: "Keep Moving!" It was during this charge that Benny received a severe wound, probably shrapnel, just below his left knee. The blow knocked him off his feet. His charging days were over. No more marching twenty-five and thirty miles per day as he described in a letter to his brother: "Blistered we commenced our march on the 11th and have been marching ever since. We start of a morning and about daylight we are about two miles from Culpeper Courthouse, about 75 miles from Richmond. We are on our way to Maryland. I expect there are two or three divisions along with us and I never saw the like of so many wagons. You can see wagons for miles. We have passed two or three battlefields. We passed where General Jackson was wounded. There are graveyards every where along the road and a great many dead horses. In some places the dead men's feet or hands are visible. They aren't buried more than six inches deep."

Benny lay on the field of battle, as family custom relates, while his comrades rushed forward. Meanwhile, the cannonading continued and Ben was struck a second time in the left eye. After this second wound, Benny, with extreme effort, crawled out of the field into a creek bed surrounded by a line of trees. This position offered him some protection. Of course Benny's family had no idea what had happened to him, but they received a letter from one of Ben's superiors, W. S. Grier on August 1, 1863. "I must commence this by offering an apology. I should have written you sooner, but when I tell you the news, I know you will excuse my negligence. In the first place, I have been steady marching for nearly two weeks and all those who were slightly wounded were sent on to Staunton, Va. Benny went on with the rest of the wounded. Mr. Wilson says he has looked everywhere but could not find him. I will speak truth because I am writing to you. I would rather have left any man in my company than Benny. He was such a good boy and never did anything worthy of reproach. A better soldier never lived. … I am fearful that he is in the hands of the Yankees. …"

Fortunately, the enemy had not captured Benny. He was recuperating at Winchester, Virginia and received excellent care from what he called his "Angel" who remained a life-long friend. A family friend, J. W. Brown visited Benny and wrote that his life was not in danger, but that amputation of his leg might be necessary to save it. Brown ended his letter by writing: "But in the event of his losing his leg and his being restored to health and home, would you not all have great reason to thank God who rules all … the thousand which are cut down and their friends never know that they were even respectably buried?"

In late September 1863, Benny had recovered enough to write his family back in Steele Creek, North Carolina. "… I have not been able to walk any yet and won't be for some time.

If I still continue to mend, it will be a good while before I am able to walk so you need not look for me home soon. I won't be able to travel for a long time. I dress it (his leg) in warm water and my eye is entirely well and is closed. I miss it very much, but nothing like I do my leg. But if I can get well, I will be very thankful that it is no worse. ..." Benny had lost both his leg and an eye!

Benny's wish for restored health was realized. By the next summer he was home receiving letters from his buddies in the eleventh regiment of the Old North State. His friend, E. M. Crowell gave him the news of the regiment and ended with this paragraph: "I suppose you have herd of Brother Sam being in the hands of the Yanks. He was taken some two weeks ago. I have not herd from him since taken. Ben, I hope you have got able to stir around through the country with yar one leg. I have never herd from you since you got home. I have been longing to write to you for some time, but have neglected it. You must write to me and give me all the news. And don't forget a fellow because he is in the army. ..."

Young Ben Coffey made it home on one leg and with a patch over one eye. Sixteen years later on February 17, 1880 he married Lucinda Robinson. This union begot Miss Morrow Coffey who married Frank Graham, who begot four children, Billy, Catherine, Melvin, and Jean Graham. It is fortunate for hundreds of thousands, perhaps millions of people around the globe that Benny Coffey, with a little help from above, pulled himself out of harm's way that hot August day in Gettysburg, Pennsylvania. Otherwise the greatest evangelist of our time, Billy Graham, might never have been born!

Fraternal Ties Are Strong

Excerpts from the *Brunswick County Bicentennial Publication*, by Gay Neale, with support from Bobby Wrenn, and excerpts from *Heroic Deeds of Noble Master Masons during the Civil War*, by Jacob Jewell

At the time of the War Between the States, Masonic Lodges were extremely influential in the affairs of men and communities. It is reasonable to note that this fraternal organization bound an entire nation to a common cause of brotherhood and service to others which often transcended allegiance to the Union or the Confederacy. Evidence of this tie that binds the hearts of men shows up in correspondence, diaries, news accounts and many similar documents that remain from that period in history. Confederate General Nathan Bedford Forrest, in the thick of his Western Theatre campaign wrote to his Masonic brother in Memphis to make sure his Lodge dues were current. This preeminent organization, which began in Europe during the Middle Ages, attracted members like George Washington, many members of the signers of the Declaration of Independence, and included thousands of soldiers of the War Between the States.

The following examples of masonry in action during the war are representative of the thousands of kind deeds done by those fraternal brothers from both the North and the South. Masons vow to provide aid to widows and orphans and to brother Masons and their families.

An Apron Saves The Archives

Robert Turnbull, of Brunswick County, Virginia was a young boy at the time when a federal unit raided that section of Virginia. Such raids struck fear in the hearts of defenseless residents. The raiders often burnt homes and businesses, stole valuable property, harassed the citizens, and destroyed official public documents. Young Robert was in the office with his father, who served as County Clerk, when news of the raid arrived. Robert's father immediately placed his Masonic apron, a symbolic article worn at all official Lodge events, on the office table in an effort to protect the precious county records. Mr. Turnbull then fled to his home with his son.

About twenty minutes after the raiders came into town a guard was sent to the Turnbull house to give the apron back to Mr. Turnbull. When the raiders left, Robert and his father rushed to the office to find papers scattered all over the floor with ink spread about. Upon inspection, however, they found nothing of value was destroyed. The soldiers had simply scattered blank sheets of paper, but left the records, dating from 1732, in tact. It was obvious that a fellow mason was in the raiding party.

Saved In The Brink Of Time

George Sandusky of Company K, 1st Regiment of the Kentucky Cavalry Volunteers was a very loyal member of the Union army when the Confederates captured him. He was so bitter against the Southern cause he determined not to reveal he was a mason, because it was common knowledge that Masonic prisoners usually received better care than non-Masonic prisoners did. In the squalid conditions of prison life, George became seriously ill and was facing eminent death. He finally told a Confederate surgeon, whom he believed to be a mason, that he also was a member of the fraternity. The surgeon replied, "My boy, why did you not tell me this before? Do you not know you are about to die?"

George replied, "Yes major, I do, but I am too loyal to my country and I intended to die rather than reveal myself, but I was driven to do so." The major then gave George a real lecture about being responsible and asking for assistance when needed. In short order, the surgeon found a lady in town who would care for George. George was removed from the prison to the lady's home where the surgeon visited each day and paid the lady for her care. George recovered, due to the diligence of his Masonic brother and was soon released in a prisoner exchange to return home.

A Miraculous Escape

L. J. Williams, of Harvard, New York was serving in the 114th Regiment of New York Volunteers when he was taken prisoner near Savannah, Georgia. L. J. had received two of the three degrees necessary to become a master mason from his home lodge in New York and wished to complete the third degree. This could not be done without the aide and instructions from fellow masons and the degree had to be conferred in an official lodge. With the assistance of his Doransville (New York) Lodge No. 464, the Zerubbabel Lodge at Savannah agreed to confer the third degree upon L. J.

One night he was taken from his prison and conducted to the Savannah Lodge. Men who wore gray uniforms while he wore a soiled and tattered blue one surrounded him. They were on opposite sides in a struggle to death, but were yet brethren in this circumstance. His Confederate brothers made him a master mason that evening and returned him to prison. Later that night, to his amazement, some men withdrew him from the prison and conveyed him by boat to the neutral ground between the two armies. The official Lodge records in Savannah reportedly list L. J. as being conferred the high degree with this notation in red ink: "On this night Brother Williams escaped from prison."

Uncommon Compassion

W. H. Morgan, a first lieutenant of the 23rd Regiment of the Kentucky Infantry Volunteers was a participant in the battle of Stone's River on New Year's Eve,

1862. His Regiment was ordered to picket duty until midnight. W. H. wrote about it: "The ground over which the contest raged all day, separated us from the Rebel pickets. Although it was supposed that all the wounded had been removed from the field and only the dead left where they fell, yet some of the supposed dead returned to consciousness during the night. The piteous cries for help (from these unfortunates) were heart-rending and chilled the blood more than the falling frost." Many of the wounded were too weak to draw the attention of their comrades for help.

Fires were prohibited and the night was very cold. To keep warm the men often huddled together (spoon fashion). W. H. was sharing a single blanket with a fellow lieutenant when he heard a peculiar cry of distress coming from the farthest side of the battlefield. Without saying a word his sleepmate arose, hunted up another mason and crawled across the field toward the voice in the night. The peculiar cry they heard was the secret Masonic distress signal. The lieutenant and his brother mason were very cautious because Confederate pickets were within yards of them. One of the Masons called softly for the wounded soldier and was promptly answered by a rebel picket who informed them that "Two of your men are lying right over there, a little way. One of them was barely able to make the call of distress and you boys couldn't hear him. So I've been repeating the signal loud enough so someone would come and help these boys." The picket then admonished the Yankees to get the wounded men away as quickly as possible since he expected relief soon and it might not be by another mason.

Chivalry Abounds

Dr. A. T. Brown of the Confederate army, 42 Regiment of the Tennessee Infantry Volunteers was in a Yankee prison when a party of foraging Yankees arrived at his home near Jackson, Mississippi. No one was home except Dr. Brown's wife and children and a Negro servant. The federals harnessed her team of horses and hitched her wagon. They then took all of the meat, 2,000 pounds, and 40 gallons of lard from the meat house. Mrs. Brown noticed a lieutenant wearing a square and compass pin, (the symbol of a mason), and made herself known as the wife of a master mason. The officer immediately rode to her side and asked: "Where did you say your husband was?" She replied he was in Johnson's Island prison in Ohio. "And you say this is all the meat and lard you have to live on?" She indicated it was her only support.

The Masonic Lieutenant wheeled his horse and told his captain he should order the men to put all the provisions back into the meat house. After some heated discussion, the captain did as the lieutenant requested. The lieutenant then asked Mrs. Brown if she knew where meat could be found elsewhere, but she refused to tell him. He then asked if he could borrow her horses and wagon and the servant. She gave him permission. The lieutenant then said, "Madam, it will be late when we return to camp and we will keep your wagon and driver in camp tonight and send him back in the morning." About ten o'clock the next morning the driver came home and handed Mrs. Brown a ten-dollar bill explaining it was to pay for him and the use of the wagon.

Saved By A Brother

Numerous incidents of condemned men being saved by a brother mason have been recorded in history. But at least on one occasion, one courageous brother mason saved thirteen men! A lieutenant and twelve men of Company M, 17th regiment of the Pennsylvania Calvary Volunteers were captured in 1864 by General Mosby's guerrillas. They were informed they would be hanged that evening. One of the prisoners was a mason and gave the distress signal. Fortunately, one of the guerrillas was a mason. He told General Mosby those men must not be killed and that if they were to be hanged, he would be hanged with them.

Tony Zeiss

The good brother was successful. The prisoners' lives were spared and they were sent to prison at Bell Island, later to Andersonville, Georgia, and were finally exchanged and sent back to their command.

An Old Man In A No-Win War
Provided By Dr. George A. Baker III

On December 17, 1860, more than 160 state delegates elected from across South Carolina met in Columbia. Three days later, they moved to Charleston and unanimously adopted the Ordinance of Secession from the Union. By the last day of 1860 the flag flying in the forts and islands guarding Charleston, with the exception of Fort Sumter, showed the white crescent moon and a palmetto tree on a dark blue background. It was the flag of South Carolina.

Later in April, 1861, Fort Sumter fell to the Confederacy and from that moment until the end of the war in 1865, South Carolina and Charleston became an obsession for President Lincoln's government — Charleston must fall and the South Carolinians must be punished. By 1863, the Federal forces had captured territory along the coast around Charleston. South Carolina's governor decided to exhaust every resource to resist an invasion of his state by Union forces. He called for the conscription of all able-bodied men to come to the aid of their homeland.

Alpheus Baker and his wife Mary Ellen must have been concerned when Alpheus, at the mature age of 38 years, was among those called to defend his home against a threat from the hated union forces of the United States. As a farmer, he was certainly concerned about who would tend to the spring crops and worried about how his wife and five children would be fed since the US Navy blockaded most manufactured and processed goods.

Alpheus was drafted into the 8th Reserve Regiment of the South Carolina Militia. He left his home in Lee County and was transported by train to Cape Chestnut near Georgetown, South Carolina for indoctrination and training. A soldier's day was never done in the training regiment. There were frequent inspections, long hours of drill, weapons firing and the like. After his initial training Alpheus was mustered into Company G of the famous 3rd South Carolina Battalion of the Light Artillery, the "Palmetto Battalion." At this time General Beauregard, defender of Charleston, increased the number of big guns around the harbor to seventy-seven. The Palmetto Battalion provided part of this "circle of fire" defense.

Alpheus was considered an old man when he was conscripted into the army and for him and all Confederate soldiers, disease was as great a threat as the enemy was. Alpheus was hospitalized in July and August of 1863, probably with cholera. Near the end of the war he was able to return to his wife and children. On New Year's Eve, 1864, he was paid for the preceding five months and twenty-one days of service for a total of $91.23. Upon arriving home, however, he found his Confederate money was almost worthless. Mary Ellen died soon after the end of the war and, following the custom of the times, Alpheus married her sister. They had four boys and a girl. Alpheus died in 1917 at the age of ninety-three. He lived to see his offspring go overseas to fight in World War I. Later his great-grandsons served in World War II, one giving his life for his country, and several great-great grandsons served in Korea and in Vietnam. None, however, served under more difficult conditions than did Alpheus Baker. No American soldier since his times has had to leave a family with no means of support in order to defend his own soil.

A Yankee Prisoner In Texas
Provided By Herb Swingle

William Ryan, great grandfather of Herb Swingle, was twenty-five years old when he enlisted in the 160th New York volunteers on September 1, 1862. As most farm boys, he went to war with little idea of what to expect about where his duty would be. He was sent by boat to New Orleans to fight in Bayou Country. After meeting the enemy in several skirmishes, he saw his first real battle at Pleasant Hill, Louisiana. He was wounded in the leg and limped off to a surgeon for treatment. Later, as he was trying to find his regiment, he was captured by Confederates and taken to Camp Ford in Tyler, Texas. This was the largest Southern Prison in the Trans-Mississippi region at the time.

William was listed as missing in action and was a prisoner of war from April to October. From William's description, Camp Ford had log walls, 18 feet high and confined ten acres of scrub land. The prison held 6,000 men. The prisoners had to make their own shelters, usually A-framed units of ½ cabin and ½ cave. These habitations, called Shebangs, held ten to twelve men. Quite often work parties would go out with their guards to cut wood for Shebang construction and for fires. These work crews had one ax for each 100 men. Their food consisted of a pint of meal and one pound of meat. The guards ate the same as the prisoners. Scurvy was rampart along with dysentery and diarrhea. Eighteen men would eat out of one pot with only one wooden spoon. Their clothes consisted of whatever was on their backs when they entered the prison. Each man boiled his clothes daily to kill the lice. As men died, others would take their clothes and shoes.

William and his comrades had to build and operate their own hospital, staffed with only one Yankee doctor. Generally, William explained, "if you got sick, you died." For entertainment, the men made and played musical instruments, had wrestling matches between regiments and played baseball games. They even published their own newspaper called the *Old Flag*.

The 465 guards from the 3rd and 15th Texas Cavalry had a tough time keeping prisoners from escaping. Indeed, bloodhounds only managed to recapture forty-six of some six hundred escapees. In all, 286 prisoners died at Camp Ford from April 1864 to April 1865. On July 4, 1865, Union troops destroyed the prison. William Ryan always remembered Camp Ford and his months of incarceration. He was paroled in October, 1864 after becoming ill from exposure and rheumatism. He was mustered out of the Union army in November 1865 in Savannah, Georgia. He received $31 for clothes, $100 bounty, and $200 for being a prisoner of war. He returned to New York, married and had seven children. He died in 1897, thirty-three years to the day he had been captured in the "Bayou Country."

About the Author

Dr. Zeiss was president of Pueblo Community College in Colorado and Central Piedmont Community College in Charlotte, North Carolina for a combined 32 years. He has authored 20 books in historical, educational, and self-improvement genres. He was named the 2005 CEO of the Year for all 1,200 community colleges in America by the Association of Community College Trustees. He was the founding Executive Director of the Museum of the Bible in Washington, D.C. 2017-18 and an educational consultant until 2022.

www.ingramcontent.com/pod-product-compliance
Lightning Source LLC
Chambersburg PA
CBHW050042080526
44586CB00014B/1413